ENDURING MYSTERIES

ATLANTIS

CHRISTOPHER BAHN

CREATIVE EDUCATION • CREATIVE PAPERBACKS

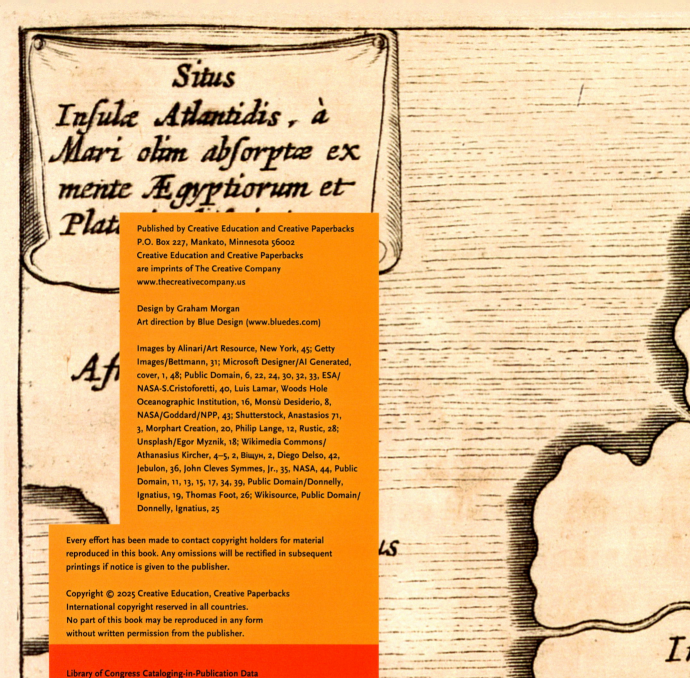

Published by Creative Education and Creative Paperbacks
P.O. Box 227, Mankato, Minnesota 56002
Creative Education and Creative Paperbacks
are imprints of The Creative Company
www.thecreativecompany.us

Design by Graham Morgan
Art direction by Blue Design (www.bluedes.com)

Images by Alinari/Art Resource, New York, 45; Getty Images/Bettmann, 31; Microsoft Designer/AI Generated, cover, 1, 48; Public Domain, 6, 22, 24, 30, 32, 33, ESA/NASA-S.Cristoforetti, 40, Luis Lamar, Woods Hole Oceanographic Institution, 16, Monsù Desiderio, 8, NASA/Goddard/NPP, 43; Shutterstock, Anastasios 71, 3, Morphart Creation, 20, Philip Lange, 12, Rustic, 28; Unsplash/Egor Myznik, 18; Wikimedia Commons/Athanasius Kircher, 4–5, 2, Віщун, 2, Diego Delso, 42, Jebulon, 36, John Cleves Symmes, Jr., 35, NASA, 44, Public Domain, 11, 13, 15, 17, 34, 39, Public Domain/Donnelly, Ignatius, 19, Thomas Foot, 26; Wikisource, Public Domain/Donnelly, Ignatius, 25

Every effort has been made to contact copyright holders for material reproduced in this book. Any omissions will be rectified in subsequent printings if notice is given to the publisher.

Copyright © 2025 Creative Education, Creative Paperbacks
International copyright reserved in all countries.
No part of this book may be reproduced in any form without written permission from the publisher.

Library of Congress Cataloging-in-Publication Data
Names: Bahn, Christopher (Children's story writer), author.
Title: Atlantis / Christopher Bahn.
Description: Mankato, Minnesota : Creative Education and Creative Paperbacks, [2025] | Series: Enduring mysteries | Includes bibliographical references and index. | Audience: Ages 10–14 years | Audience: Grades 7–9 | Summary: "An investigative approach to the mystery surrounding Atlantis for age 12 and up, from historical accounts and popular myths to hard facts and evidence. Includes a glossary, index, sidebars, and further resources"—Provided by publisher.
Identifiers: LCCN 2024015968 (print) | LCCN 2024015969 (ebook) | ISBN 9798889892854 (library binding) | ISBN 9781682776513 (paperback) | ISBN 9798889893967 (ebook)
Subjects: LCSH: Atlantis (Legendary place)—Juvenile literature.
Classification: LCC GN751 .B25 2025 (print) | LCC GN751 (ebook) | DDC 398.23/4—dc23/eng/20240527
LC record available at https://lccn.loc.gov/2024015968
LC ebook record available at https://lccn.loc.gov/2024015969

Printed in China

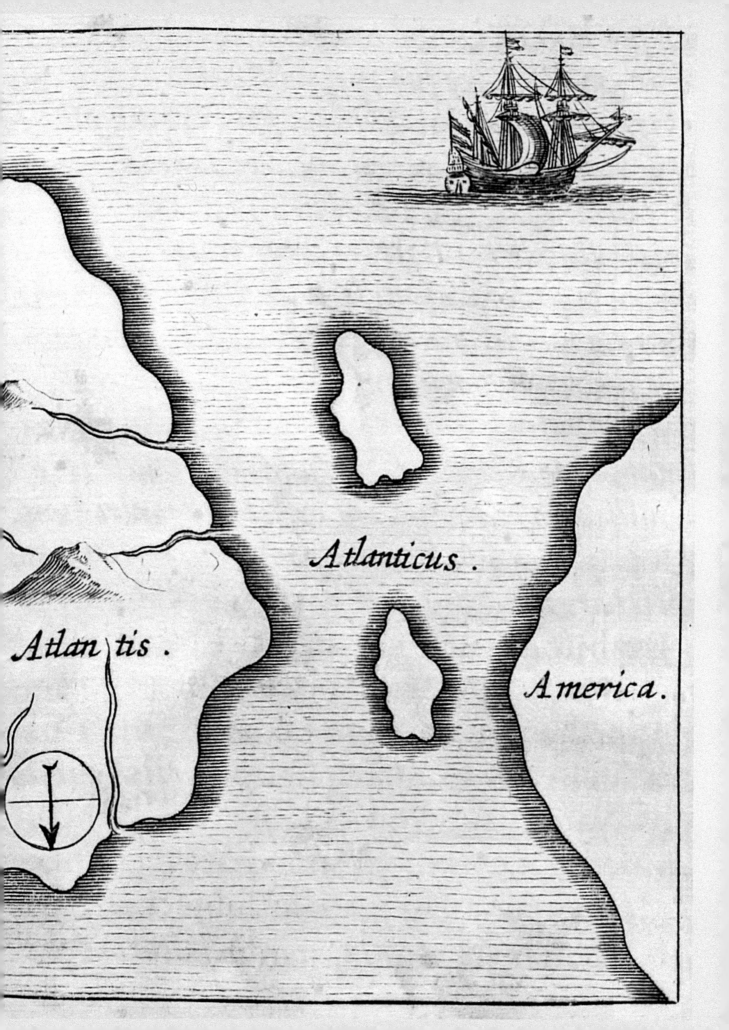

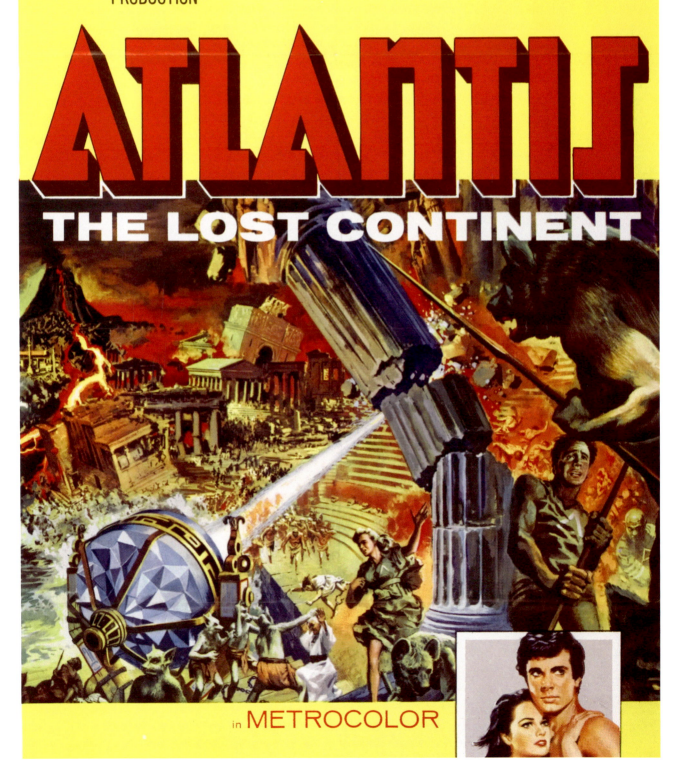

CONTENTS

Introduction 9

Atlantis, According to Plato 10

Story Revival 21

Pop Culture, Psychic Culture 29

Today and Tomorrow 37

Field Notes 46

Selected Bibliography 47

Websites 47

Index 48

INTRODUCTION

OPPOSITE: An artist's rendering from the mid-1600s of the fall of Atlantis

A strange rumble rolled beneath the earth under Atlantis. No sooner had people begun to ask one another what it might be than the rumble became a deafening thunder. The ground split apart. The shimmering palaces of cut stone and finely crafted waterways heaved, split, and fell, burying people and other structures. Dust and smoke obscured the sun. People groped about in the chaos, looking for loved ones or a route to safety. Then the surrounding sea, which had drawn away from shore when the earthquake struck, rushed back in, rose up, and crashed over the land. Those who had tried to flee in boats struggled to paddle or sail through wave after giant wave.

By nightfall, all was quiet, but the sea now covered what had been one of Earth's greatest civilizations. A small number of survivors sailed off over the calming waters. They didn't know where they might find a home. They didn't know if they would ever again enjoy the peace, security, and achievement they had had in Atlantis. Their entire world had been lost in a day. But ever since then, for thousands of years, humans have been trying to find Atlantis, in what has become a quest for an idea as much as a place.

ATLANTIS, ACCORDING TO PLATO

OPPOSITE: Ancient philosophers such as Plato were skilled thinkers, speakers, writers, and storytellers.

Although the tale of the glittering ancient culture of Atlantis has intrigued people for thousands of years, the central part of the story rests on a surprisingly narrow foundation. There is only one ancient source for the Atlantis myth: Plato, a Greek **philosopher** who lived from 428 to 348 B.C.E. Plato was a student of Socrates, who is regarded as the father of **Western** philosophy. Plato himself is considered one of the most important thinkers of ancient Greece. He told the story of Atlantis in two of his writings, *Timaeus* and *Critias*.

In these writings, Plato says that Atlantis was an island kingdom that existed about 9,000 years in his past—more than 11,000 years before present day. It was named for the Titan Atlas. So was the Atlantic Ocean. Plato tells of a war between Athens—the city where Plato

lived—and the kings of Atlantis, which he says was "greater in extent than Libya and Asia." The people of Atlantis lived in enlightenment, accomplishment, wealth, and power. Atlanteans ruled an empire next to the Pillars of Heracles, beyond which was "a great ocean of which the Mediterranean Sea was only the harbor." Many modern writers assume this is a reference to the Strait of Gibraltar—the narrow, watery gate between Spain and Morocco—and the vast Atlantic Ocean to its west. The Atlantean empire, says Plato, included areas in Tyrrhenia (modern Italy), Libya, and Egypt.

In Plato's story, like many stories from Greek mythology, the gods were real. They took a direct hand in the course of human civilization. Many Greek cities had patron gods as part of their founding myths. Atlantis's was Poseidon, god of the sea and earthquakes. Poseidon married a human named Cleito. She had grown up on the island. Poseidon built a palace for her on a peak, surrounded by rings of water and stone walls. Poseidon and Cleito had five sets of twin sons, each

OPPOSITE: The Rock of Gibraltar, on the tip of the Iberian Peninsula, is considered one of the Pillars of Heracles.

of whom ruled over a portion of Atlantis. The firstborn of the first set of twins was Atlas, who became king. Their family ruled the island for many generations.

The island was renowned for its beauty. It was mountainous near the seacoast, but in the center near the city stretched a vast, fertile plain that Plato says was 340 miles (547 kilometers) long by 230 miles (370 km) wide. This plain had been carefully reworked over generations by Atlantean civil engineers. They had crafted a complex network of canals and aqueducts. The walled harbors of Atlantis were always busy with people and vessels. Atlantis had a standing army of 10,000 chariots, 1,200 ships, and more than 100,000 soldiers.

The people of Atlantis, said Plato, were not only wealthy and comfortable but also accomplished in war, art, and government. They

THE TITAN ATLAS

OPPOSITE: In Greek mythology, Zeus is the god of the sky and ruler over all other gods.

were blessed by a gentle, productive climate. The land provided them with many natural resources, including wood, precious metals, and (thanks to Poseidon) both hot and cold springs of water. There were rich groves of fruit trees and herds of elephants. There was great wealth from mining, including a mysterious metal called orichalcum that was almost as precious as gold. Bridges and walls were built of red, black, and white rock quarried from the island. Atlanteans learned how to make tools of iron and invented bronze, which they used to make axes, ship parts, decorations, and saws. They built public baths, gardens, exercise palaces, temples, and a horse-racing track. Their location—a crossroads on the sea—brought them visitors, knowledge, and goods from all around the world. At the center of the island, temples honoring Poseidon and Cleito were built of gold and silver. The rulers of Atlantis would gather at the main temple every few years to discuss laws, settle disputes, and pay tribute to Poseidon.

For many years, the Atlanteans were gentle and wise. They lived in a **utopia**. But then they changed. They became corrupt and warlike—Plato wrote that they were "full of avarice and unrighteous power." They sought to enslave the cities around them. The noble Athenians eventually led a battle against the Atlanteans and won, freeing the cities Atlantis had conquered.

Zeus, the king of the Greek gods, called all the gods together to decide how to punish Atlantis for its crimes. Then, Plato said, "violent earthquakes and floods" rocked the island, "and in a single day and night of misfortune, all [the] warlike men sank into the earth, and

ATLANTIS AFLOAT

Atlantis has always had a strong association with undersea mysteries. It's no wonder that it has lent its name to 3 research craft of the Woods Hole Oceanographic Institution over the past 80 years. The first *Atlantis* operated by the Massachusetts-based institute was a 144-foot (44-meter) two-masted boat. It sailed nearly 196,000 miles (315,431 km) from 1931 to 1966. It was the first ship built specifically for explorations dedicated to marine biology, geology, and oceanography. *Atlantis II* succeeded it. It logged more miles than any other research vessel ever, racking up 1 million miles (1.6 million km) and 468 cruises in 33 years. It supported the piloted underwater vessel *Alvin*, which explored the *Titanic* wreck as well as major geologic features on the seafloor. In 1996, it was sold to a private firm for use in fishery research in the Pacific. After *Atlantis II*, Woods Hole reverted to the name *Atlantis* for its next research vessel, which is owned by the U.S. Navy and was launched in 1997. It totes the *Alvin* around the world, primarily studying deep-sea volcanoes. None of the ships, nor *Alvin*, has ever found a lost continent.

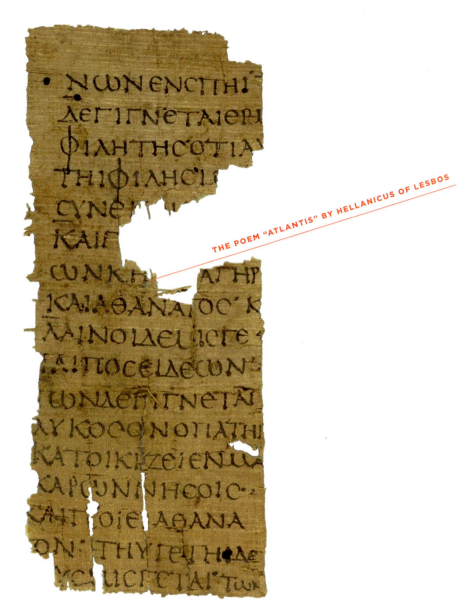

THE POEM "ATLANTIS" BY HELLANICUS OF LESBOS

the island of Atlantis disappeared in the depths of the sea." All that remained was "an impassable barrier of mud."

Plato's story has intrigued people for thousands of years. Historians, **archaeologists**, **geologists**, and other scholars have sought to uncover the truth. But was Plato's story meant to be believed? For one thing, Plato was a philosopher, not a historian. Socrates, Plato, and other philosophers thought deeply and raised important questions about what kind of society might be best for all people. They discussed issues of justice, art, truth, and government. In works such as *The Republic*, Plato explored those ideas by using invented conversations, or dialogues,

ATLANTIS, ACCORDING TO PLATO

17

RIGHT: Ruins of the Minoan Palace in the city of Knossos, Greece, may have connections to Atlantis.

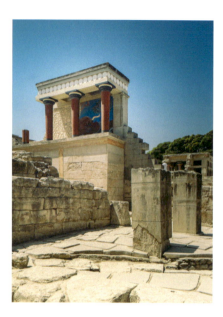

between himself and several other philosophers, including Socrates. The dialogue form was a way to present the many sides of, and perspectives on, an idea or issue by identifying key challenges and revealing how problems might best be resolved. Plato wrote dozens of dialogues, including *Timaeus* and *Critias*, the sources for Atlantis. Plato may simply have invented Atlantis as a way to make a point in a philosophical discussion.

Even if the story were true, it probably came from an oral tradition passed down through the generations, like the famous *Odyssey* and *Iliad* stories of Homer, and was not written down until Plato. There are many reasons to doubt its accuracy. Mark Adams, author of the book *Meet Me in Atlantis*, calls Plato's story "messy and confusing." He notes that it probably would not hold up in a modern court of law. Even Plato acknowledges he gets the story fifth-hand: Plato is told by his friend Critias, who gets it from his grandfather and great-grandfather, who got it from the statesman Solon (630–560 B.C.E.), who learned it from Egyptian priests who lived some 200 years before Plato himself.

Could Atlantis have been real? Many scholars have tried to prove that it was. Where could such a huge island have been? Some people have placed it in the Atlantic Ocean, suggesting such islands as the Azores, or the Canary Islands, which lie in the Atlantic west of Gibraltar. If Atlantis had been as big as Plato claimed, could it really have just sunk, been flooded, or simply vanished? And could the disaster have taken place in only one day? Those are all parts of the puzzle.

Scientists, for the most part, have scoffed at Plato's story. However, modern archaeology has found evidence of a sophisticated civilization called the Minoans on islands near Greece. They were wiped out by a volcano and earthquake centuries before Plato—but they did not live as far back in time as Plato said the people of Atlantis did. Furthermore, landmasses of that size simply do not vanish in a day. Even an earthquake and tsunami wouldn't remove a large island, concealing it so thoroughly that no one would have found any trace for thousands of years.

Yet Atlantis continues to fire the human imagination. "Atlantis is not merely a territory swallowed up by the sea, like, say, the land formerly joining England to France," writes British cultural historian Geoffrey Ashe, author of *Atlantis: Lost Lands, Ancient Wisdom*. "It is not merely a theme for geographic debate, or volcanic or **seismic** speculation. Its spell is inherent, compelling, and strong enough to lend credibility to theories that are often incredible."

AN UNPROVEN MAP OF ATLANTIS

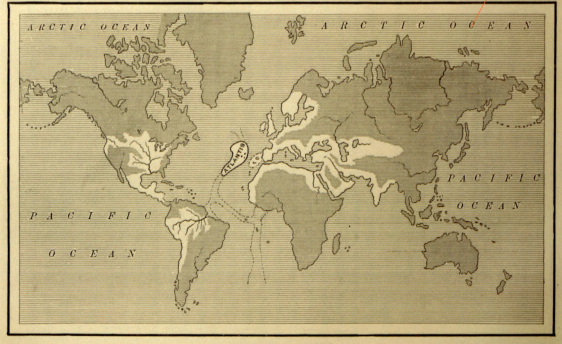

THE EMPIRE OF ATLANTIS.

STORY REVIVAL

The story of Atlantis is not known from any earlier source than Plato. Aristotle, Plato's student and an important philosopher in his own right, dismissed the idea that Atlantis was real. He seemed to suggest that Plato made the whole thing up with the remark, "He who invented it also destroyed it." L. Sprague de Camp's book *Lost Continents* (first published in 1954) is a **skeptical** examination of the history of the Atlantis myth. It says that after a few further appearances in ancient Greek writings, the myth disappears from the historical record and "nothing more is heard of it for many centuries." But that didn't kill off interest in the sunken city. Far from it: The myth of Atlantis persists to this day. It has inspired hundreds of authors and explorers to seek out its truth any way possible—sometimes in solid science and archaeology, sometimes in wild speculation and fantasy.

The discovery of the New World in the 1490s by Europeans gave fresh energy to the story of Atlantis. Was the vast "new" land the lost Atlantis? Had Atlanteans ventured there and left any traces of their advanced

OPPOSITE: Atlantis may have existed only inside the mind of Plato.

OPPOSITE: Francis Bacon's fictional island, Bensalem, was home to a utopian society much like that of Atlantis.

civilization? Didn't the discovery of one "new world" suggest that Atlantis, supposedly lost long before, might still be out there, somewhere?

The imaginations of European philosophers and artists found great inspiration in the story of Atlantis, which they built on in new works. Sir Francis Bacon (1561–1626), an English statesman and scholar, published a novel in 1624 called *The New Atlantis*. In it, he, like Plato, described an island of enlightened, peace-loving inhabitants who enjoyed freedom of religion and advanced scientific education. The island, called Bensalem, was located in what is today the Pacific Ocean. There was no violent end to this island, however, as with Atlantis. And the story was more a tale of a new beginning, in which some stranded English sailors land on Bensalem and establish a new society. Bacon was influential in the founding of the American colonies, and the book is often seen as Bacon's vision of how the New World could be developed.

Bacon turned the spotlight from a lost continent to a newly discovered one, but the notion of a place where people once lived amid splendor and justice was still popular. But where was it? The location varies from story to story. The island's home waters have been suggested to be in the Pacific Ocean and in the Mediterranean and Caribbean Seas. It's also been traced to the continents of Africa, South America, and Europe. One European location may be the most incredible: Sweden.

Olof Rudbeck (1630–1702) was a 17th-century medical professor at Sweden's Uppsala University who specialized in the human circulatory system. But he was far better known for his 3,000-page, 4-volume work, first published in 1679, that presented the case for Atlantis having been a precursor to Uppsala, his own city. Rudbeck matched Plato's descriptions of Atlantis with the geography of Uppsala. Then he went even further. He found evidence of a pagan temple and a horse-racing track. He also

OPPOSITE: "Dolphin's Ridge," known today as the Mid-Atlantic Ridge, is thought by some to be a remnant of Atlantis.

developed a theory that the Swedish language, because it had been spoken by Atlanteans who had lived in ancient Uppsala, was the human race's mother tongue. The Pillars of Heracles were not, Rudbeck claimed, at the Strait of Gibraltar, beyond which many ancient peoples had sailed. They were the Oresund, a cold and treacherous channel between Denmark and Sweden. Finally, Rudbeck argued that the ancient name for Sweden, *Atland*, was perhaps the clearest link to Atlantis yet.

Rudbeck was roundly criticized, even in his own circle of scholars, for faulty science. But the American historian David King asserts that Rudbeck did some good scientific research along the way. Rudbeck recognized that layers of rock and soil could indicate the age of items found in the ground. Rudbeck also built ships to show how the legendary Greek hero Jason could have sailed from Greece through Europe to Sweden. By doing so, Rudbeck established a type of archaeology that tested theories with actual experience.

In the late 19th century, Atlantis became something of a craze. French author Jules Verne, considered to be the father of science fiction, featured it in his 1870 novel *Twenty Thousand Leagues under the Sea*. Then, in 1882, Atlantis got a new lease on life with the publication of a book called *Atlantis: The Antediluvian World* (*antediluvian* meaning "before a great flood"). The book's author, an American named Ignatius Donnelly (1831–1901), was something of a legendary character himself: a writer, speaker, newspaper editor, amateur scientist, and political reformer. Donnelly had tried to establish a utopian community in Minnesota in the late 1850s called Nininger. The effort failed, but Donnelly

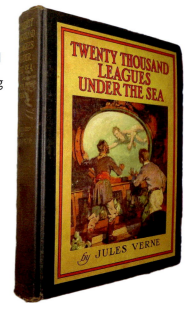

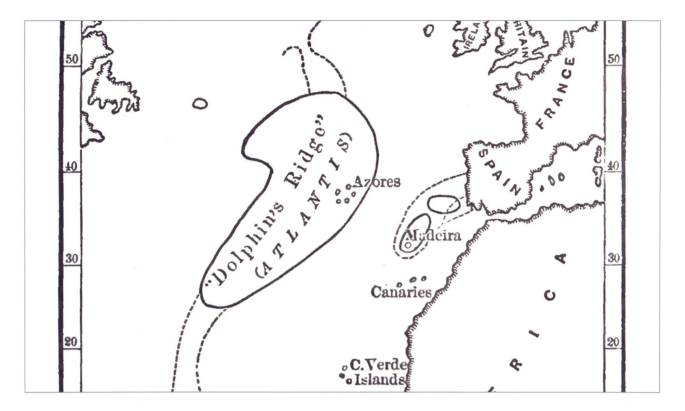

remained fascinated by the concept. In 1878, after nearly 20 years in government, including serving as lieutenant governor of Minnesota and three terms in the U.S. Congress, Donnelly wrote and published his work on Atlantis. With it, he achieved far more recognition than he'd ever had in politics.

Treating Plato's story as "veritable history," Donnelly probably did more to popularize the Atlantis story than Plato himself, describing it as the birthplace of all humanity. Atlantis, he wrote, was "the region where man first rose from a state of barbarism to civilization." It was a great island in the Atlantic Ocean surrounded by islands spreading east and west like "stepping-stones." This location allowed its people, the source of all the races and "the founders of nearly all our arts and sciences," to spread across the planet. Donnelly used facts such as the presence of bananas in both South America and Africa to support the argument that a landmass or system of islands must have connected the two continents. Atlanteans, he said, were thus able to distribute their ironworking and **embalming** skills; the bronze, gunpowder, and magnets they'd invented; cotton, grain, and mills; and their signature architecture, including pyramids. According to Donnelly, the innovations that had previously

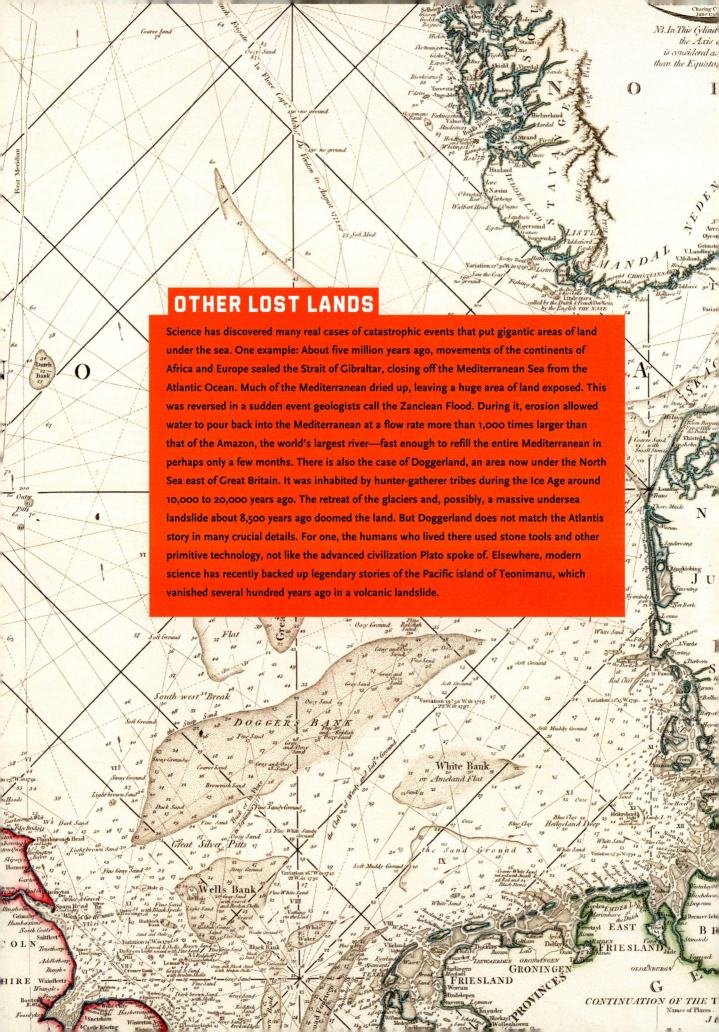

OTHER LOST LANDS

Science has discovered many real cases of catastrophic events that put gigantic areas of land under the sea. One example: About five million years ago, movements of the continents of Africa and Europe sealed the Strait of Gibraltar, closing off the Mediterranean Sea from the Atlantic Ocean. Much of the Mediterranean dried up, leaving a huge area of land exposed. This was reversed in a sudden event geologists call the Zanclean Flood. During it, erosion allowed water to pour back into the Mediterranean at a flow rate more than 1,000 times larger than that of the Amazon, the world's largest river—fast enough to refill the entire Mediterranean in perhaps only a few months. There is also the case of Doggerland, an area now under the North Sea east of Great Britain. It was inhabited by hunter-gatherer tribes during the Ice Age around 10,000 to 20,000 years ago. The retreat of the glaciers and, possibly, a massive undersea landslide about 8,500 years ago doomed the land. But Doggerland does not match the Atlantis story in many crucial details. For one, the humans who lived there used stone tools and other primitive technology, not like the advanced civilization Plato spoke of. Elsewhere, modern science has recently backed up legendary stories of the Pacific island of Teonimanu, which vanished several hundred years ago in a volcanic landslide.

been attributed to other civilizations (such as Egypt's) could instead be traced to Atlantis. Even though no one had ever found any physical evidence of Atlantis, Donnelly wrote, the fact that people remembered and continued to tell the story was proof enough that it once existed.

American critic J. M. Tyree said in 2005 that Donnelly's vision was based on "bad math, misreading the archaeological record, and mistaking ancient myths for veiled historical chronicles." He called Donnelly "probably the greatest crackpot that ever lived." Nevertheless, Donnelly's writing had a huge influence on Atlantis in popular culture. *Atlantis: The Antediluvian World* became a best seller and made him a celebrity.

The popularity of Donnelly's book gave rise to a wave of Atlantis **pseudoscience**. From the 1880s on, other explorers claimed they had found Atlantis. French geographer Etienne Felix Berlioux (1828–1910) said he had located ruins of Atlantis near the Atlas Mountains in Morocco. This was the first of several theories that placed Atlantis in Africa in the 13th century B.C.E. Other researchers offered variations on that idea. In 1926, French archaeologist Claude Roux (1872–1961) wrote that Atlantis had been a thriving civilization on the Mediterranean coast of northwestern Africa before its marshy environment turned to desert. Count Byron Khun de Prorok (1896–1954) was an American who was regarded by both professional archaeologists and native peoples as a **tomb-raider**. He linked Atlantis to his 1925 discovery of the tomb of Tin Hinan, the legendary female leader of the Tuareg tribe in the Sahara Desert. Around the same time, German archaeologists also "discovered" Atlantis in Africa, amidst Tunisian ruins. Whether underwater or on land in a now-deserted place, the true location of Atlantis continues to elude even the most persistent seekers.

POP CULTURE, PSYCHIC CULTURE

OPPOSITE: Submarines in search of Atlantis feature in countless science fiction stories around the world.

One way to measure how deeply the story of Atlantis has affected the human imagination is to see how often it turns up in popular culture. Jules Verne was one of the first writers to imagine what a "real-life" encounter with Atlantis might be like. In *Twenty Thousand Leagues under the Sea*, the character of Captain Nemo captures a marine biologist and takes him on a submarine voyage through the underwater remains of Atlantis. Another French author, Pierre Benoit, took his countryman Berlioux's idea that Atlantis had been in Morocco and made it into a novel called *Atlantida*. Benoit's Atlantis was populated by a queen who lured men into her world, killed them, and had them embalmed and made into statues. The novel, published in 1919, became so popular that was made into a movie at least seven times.

OPPOSITE: Although labeled a fraud by some, Madame Blavatsky did open dialogues about religion and spirituality.

Sir Arthur Conan Doyle, the Scottish author best known for creating the detective character Sherlock Holmes, built his 1929 novel *The Maracot Deep* around the story of the search for Atlantis. American author Edgar Rice Burroughs's durable hero Tarzan visited a lost colony of Atlantis in *Tarzan and the Jewels of Opar.* Robert E. Howard's Kull the Conqueror was the hero of several of the writer's sword-and-sorcery tales, which followed Kull's exploits as the king of Atlantis in 100,000 B.C.E. Horror writer H. P. Lovecraft drew on the myth of a sunken city for R'lyeh, home of the titanic monster Cthulhu (KLUL-hloo). And J. R. R. Tolkien, author of *The Lord of the Rings*, based his land of Númenor on the idea of Atlantis as an ancient paradise destroyed and sunken by human overconfidence.

Many films feature characters who survive the destruction of Atlantis. The 2001 Disney animated science fiction film *Atlantis: The Lost Empire* is an example. Atlantis has also been a favorite theme in video games, most notably in the landmark 1992 game *Indiana Jones and the Fate of Atlantis* and in *Tomb Raider*, which is partly set in Atlantis. In comic books, both Aquaman from DC Comics and Namor the Sub-Mariner from Marvel are well-known to readers as rulers of

thriving undersea kingdoms of Atlantis. Both have appeared in blockbuster superhero movies in recent years. Writer Neil Gaiman also places Atlantis in his comic books, novels, and graphic novels. Even Donald Duck and Doctor Who have visited Atlantis!

Because Atlantis's existence has never been proven—or disproven—the idea of a lost civilization has taken on mythic qualities. Especially after Ignatius Donnelly, the idea of Atlantis attracted believers in magic, **occult** philosophy, psychic phenomena, and other fringe theories. These writers have used Atlantis to fill in the blanks or provide alternative explanations to scientific theories about evolution, the movement of continents, and cultural connections.

While Donnelly infused a more scientific tone into his writings about Atlantis, a contemporary of his, Russian-born Helena Petrovna Blavatsky (1831–91) wasn't as disciplined. Blavatsky was a circus bareback rider, piano teacher, and religious seeker who traveled widely and lived near India. She cofounded the Theosophical Society in 1875. Its mission was to promote the search for truth by combining religion, science, **reincarnation**, and other topics. Blavatsky became a U.S. citizen in 1878 and was widely known as Madame Blavatsky. She claimed she had learned about Atlantis from secret writings and occult revelations handed down through followers of the Mahatmas. The Mahatmas were advanced beings who had lived for many centuries

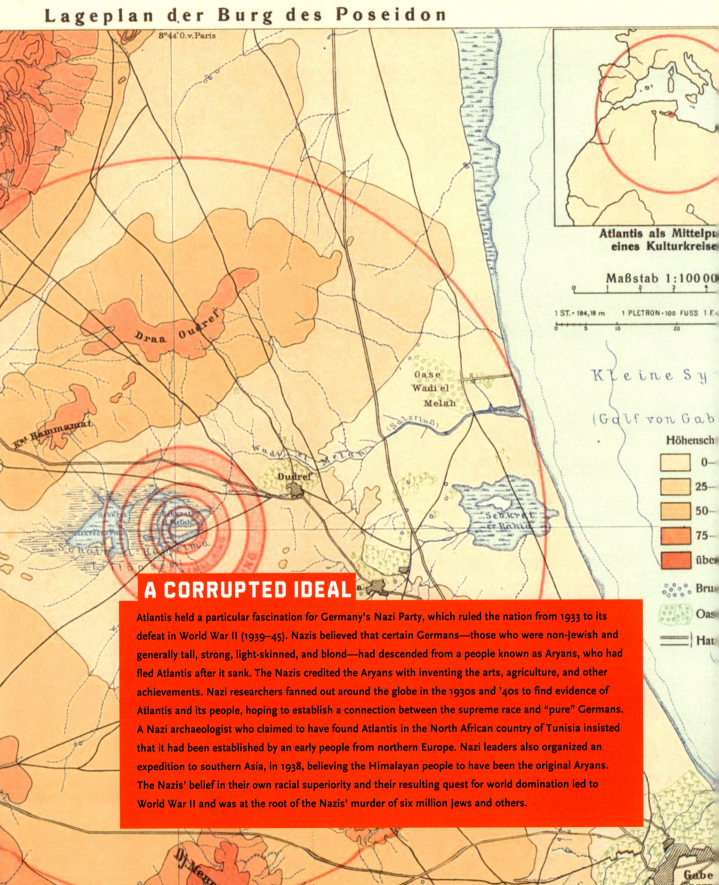

A CORRUPTED IDEAL

Atlantis held a particular fascination for Germany's Nazi Party, which ruled the nation from 1933 to its defeat in World War II (1939–45). Nazis believed that certain Germans—those who were non-Jewish and generally tall, strong, light-skinned, and blond—had descended from a people known as Aryans, who had fled Atlantis after it sank. The Nazis credited the Aryans with inventing the arts, agriculture, and other achievements. Nazi researchers fanned out around the globe in the 1930s and '40s to find evidence of Atlantis and its people, hoping to establish a connection between the supreme race and "pure" Germans. A Nazi archaeologist who claimed to have found Atlantis in the North African country of Tunisia insisted that it had been established by an early people from northern Europe. Nazi leaders also organized an expedition to southern Asia, in 1938, believing the Himalayan people to have been the original Aryans. The Nazis' belief in their own racial superiority and their resulting quest for world domination led to World War II and was at the root of the Nazis' murder of six million Jews and others.

EDGAR CAYCE

in remote Asian areas and used **telepathy** to enlighten certain favored people. In her 1888 book *The Secret Doctrine*, published six years after Donnelly's work, she asserted that Atlanteans were the fourth human race to have existed and that they had lived during the age of dinosaurs. She argued that the centuries-old fascination with dragons was possible proof that humans had coexisted with huge reptiles. She also strongly promoted an Atlantis alternative known as Lemuria.

Austrian engineer Hanns Hörbiger (1860–1931) took the idea of Atlantis and used it to develop an astronomical theory that extended even farther back in time. He argued that Earth once had many ice-covered moons. These satellites orbited at varying distances until they were reeled in by the pull of Earth's gravity, causing earthquakes, volcanoes, showers of ice, and devastating tides. The ice and the rising seas were the reasons, Hörbiger said, that people in Atlantis and later civilizations built their cities and monuments on high ground. Such an explanation contradicted Plato's description of Atlantis as having plains near sea level. It did, however, serve to link South American pyramid-builders and the people of the Himalayas with Atlantis.

Edgar Cayce (1877–1945) was an American who claimed to be able to see Atlantis by using special powers. As a young man, Cayce had temporarily lost the power of speech as a result of illness but found he could speak while under hypnosis. He also discovered that he could diagnose people's illnesses and recommend cures by going into a trance. Later, he turned his powers toward Atlantis. He gave lectures describing a civilization that possessed aircraft, electricity,

MOUNT SHASTA

and something like atomic energy. Cayce asserted that half the world's people were reincarnated Atlanteans and claimed that Atlanteans from long ago spoke to him. He also foretold that part of Atlantis would be found in the late 1960s in the Bahamas, off the east coast of Florida. About that time, and again in the early 1970s, expeditions identified underwater rock formations beneath the sea that seemed to resemble the remains of buildings, streets, and columns. But oceanographers countered that rock ledges near beaches often break naturally in straight lines and right angles, making them look like constructed materials.

The influence of Atlantis has continued to connect many strands of belief, fear, culture, and scientific theory. California's Mount Shasta has a strong Atlantis connection in the modern world among believers in the occult. The mountain's connection to the Atlantis myth has its roots in Frederick Spencer Oliver's 1883 book *Dweller on Two Planets*. Oliver claimed the book was a true story. He said he had been physically compelled to write by a spirit named Phylos the Thibetan who took control of Oliver's hands. Phylos's story tells of the fall of Atlantis, here an ancient city of high technology, and the descendants who came to live as a society of mystics inside Mount Shasta. In 1987, believers in New Age thinking thought that an unusual alignment of the planets, called the Harmonic Convergence, would usher in a time of great spiritual possibility. Thousands of people gathered at Mount Shasta to take advantage of the spiritual energy they believed existed there.

Another belief, dating back to the early 19th century and championed by American John Cleves Symmes (1780–1829), claimed that Earth was hollow. Later writers such as Raymond Bernard (1903–65) expanded on this to say that the survivors of Atlantis had moved to the center of the planet. There, they supposedly flew around in flying saucers that sometimes emerged from the poles. Could Atlantis be deep beneath us? Was it transformed into a UFO base run by alien navigators who kidnap Earth-dwellers and reprogram them for Atlantean purposes? Science says no. But some still insist it's possible.

LIGHT GIVES LIGHT, TO LIGHT DISCOVER—"AD INFINITUM."

ST. LOUIS, (Missouri Territory,)
North America, April 10, *A. D.* 1818.

TO ALL THE WORLD!

I declare the earth is hollow, and habitable within; containing a number of solid concentrick spheres, one within the other, and that it is open at the poles 12 or 16 degrees; I pledge my life in support of this truth, and am ready to explore the hollow, if the world will support and aid me in the undertaking.

Jno. Cleves Symmes

Of Ohio, late Captain of Infantry.

In 1818, U.S. Army captain John Symmes tried to recruit 100 people to explore Earth's hollow interior with him.

... for the press, a Treatise on the principles of matter, wherein I show proofs of the above positions, account for various phenomena, and disclose *Doctor Darwin's Golden Secret.*

My terms, are the patronage of this and the new worlds.

I dedicate to my Wife and her ten Children.

I select *Doctor S. L. Mitchell, Sir H. Davy* and *Baron Alex. de Humboldt,* as my protectors.

I ask one hundred brave companions, well equipped, to start from Siberia in the fall season, with Reindeer and slays, on the ice of the frozen sea; I engage we find warm and rich land, stocked with thrifty vegetables and animals if not men, on reaching one degree northward of latitude 82; we will return in the succeeding spring.   J. C. S.

TODAY AND TOMORROW

OPPOSITE: An ancient statue of the Greek god of the sea, Poseidon, found in Knossos, Greece

For more than 2,000 years, Atlantis remained just an idea—located beyond the familiar world, lost to history. But toward the end of the 19th century, Atlantis, like a ghost materializing, seemed to return to the physical realm.

In 1878, Minos Kalokairinos (1843–1907), a member of a wealthy family of Greek merchants with a deep interest in archaeology, turned his attention to ruins at Knossos, a city on the island of Crete. Kalokairinos found painted walls and pottery, and in 1894 shared his discoveries with Sir Arthur Evans (1851–1941), a British journalist and archaeologist. Three years later, Evans purchased the land containing the ruins and began digging. Over the course of 30 years, Evans and dozens of workers uncovered a 10-acre (4-hectare), 1,300-room palace and estate. Evans declared it to have been the likely palace of King Minos (Kalokairinos's namesake, by coincidence), a Cretan king and mythical son of the god Zeus and the Phoenician princess Europa.

OPPOSITE: In Greek mythology, the hero Theseus killed the minotaur living inside Minos's maze.

According to mythology, Minos's wife, Pasiphae, conceived a son with a bull. Minos arranged to have the half-man creature with the head of a bull—known as a minotaur—kept in a maze beneath his palace. There he fed it human children captured from conquered lands. Evans's workers were jolted when they uncovered the bust of a bull with red eyes that moved (without battery power)!

The ruins at Knossos astonished the world not because of their age or strangeness but because of the advanced technological skill they revealed. Buildings at Knossos exhibited stones that had been cut to precision with bronze saws, earthquake-resistant timber framing, and interior spaces designed to let in light and increase air circulation. There were sophisticated water management systems, including hot and cold water and sewage removal.

More recently, in 1968, archaeology professor Spyridon Marinatos (1901–74) excavated a site on the Greek island of Santorini—called Thera in ancient times—located 100 miles (161 km) north of Crete. At a site called Akrotiri, workers uncovered a magnificent complex. It was similar to Knossos, with buildings that were several stories tall and extensive paintings including images of bulls, African animals, and ships.

Scholars came to call the people who built and lived in these capitals as Minoans—subjects of Minos, builders of a civilization hundreds of years more advanced than Greece. The Minoans had extensive trading contacts in Egypt, where many of their artifacts have been found. One thing the Minoans didn't leave behind was a known language, although we know of two systems of writing they invented. While their advanced architecture, artistic skills, and accomplished seamanship suggest they might have been the people of Plato's Atlantis, the story of the Minoans' end makes the case even stronger.

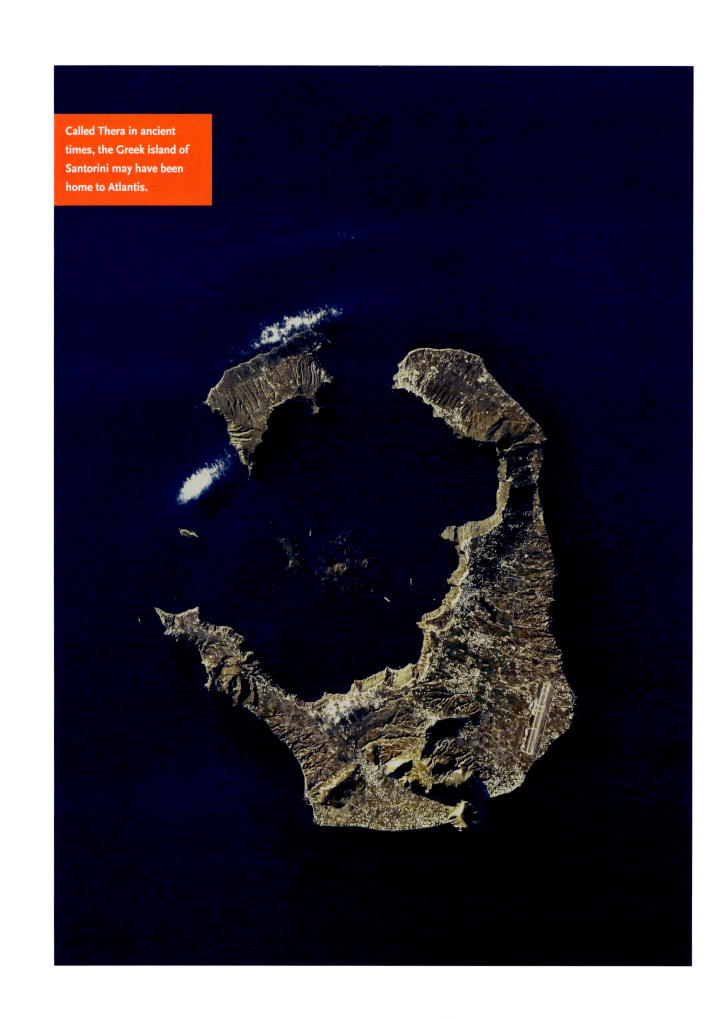

Called Thera in ancient times, the Greek island of Santorini may have been home to Atlantis.

Around 1600 B.C.E., a volcanic eruption destroyed most of the island of Thera. It left only a fringe of land arranged in a horseshoe around a central underwater crater. Experts describe the eruption as having been one million times more powerful than the atomic bomb that destroyed Hiroshima, Japan, in World War II. Alternatively, it was 10 times as powerful as the volcano that blew apart the Indonesian island of Krakatoa in 1888, killing 36,000 people and darkening the skies with so much ash that global temperatures dropped for the next 5 years. The Thera volcano buried Akrotiri in ash and rock. It generated perhaps dozens of tsunamis, which quickly slammed into neighboring Crete, destroying Knossos. Scientists say that some of the waves were as high as 27 feet (9 m), possibly capable of the destruction Plato described in his story of Atlantis. Professor Nicholas Tschoegl and others have noted that if we assume that Plato exaggerated the size and the age of Atlantis by a factor of 10—from 9,000 years to 900, in other words—then the time period and the size of the island are near-exact matches for the Theran eruption and the area of Crete where the palace of Knossos stood.

So, was Atlantis on Crete? Or was it on Thera, now called Santorini? Was it somewhere else entirely? If the Pillars of Heracles are today's Strait of Gibraltar, then perhaps Atlantis was out in the Atlantic Ocean. Or was it in the Pacific? Antarctica? In Africa or Scandinavia? Researchers, promoters, dreamers, and others have not rested in pursuit of an answer.

In 2004, an American researcher using deep-water **sonar** claimed to find Atlantis about a mile (1.6 km) beneath the Mediterranean Sea

DOÑANA NATIONAL PARK BEACH

between Syria and Cyprus. However, further review suggested the findings were merely sea sediments. Recent attention has swung back west across the Mediterranean to the Strait of Gibraltar. In 2005, a team of Spanish archaeologists began investigating evidence from satellite photos. There appeared to be buildings and concentric circles—as known from Plato's Atlantis—buried near a beach in Doñana, a national park and Europe's largest wetlands area, northwest of the strait on the southern coast of Spain. American professor Richard Freund joined that project and in 2011 claimed he had found conclusive evidence that the structures, though 60 miles (97 km) inland, were remnants of Atlantis. He calculated that survivors had fled the destruction and founded cities far inland across Spain. Freund's revelations were hotly disputed by the Spanish researchers. They said he had jumped to wild conclusions based on their work. But no matter—the search for Atlantis is likely to continue, energized by new technology.

Marinatos, who in the late 1960s excavated the Minoan splendors on Santorini, once said, "Still the best archaeological tool is the shovel. It works well and does not speak." He was saying as much about rivalries in the field as he was about the basic, careful digging central

UNDERWATER LANDMASS

Most geologists believe Atlantis could not have been destroyed by an earthquake, volcano, or tsunami as quickly as the stories say it was. Cities and other relatively small areas have sometimes been wiped out suddenly by such events, but never a continent the size of the legendary Atlantis. Did it sink? Landmasses do sink, but the process takes millions of years, so if humans—who have been around far less time than that—lived on Atlantis, it should still be around. Similarly, rising sea levels could not have topped the peaks of Atlantis during humans' time on Earth. The underwater Mid-Atlantic Ridge, which runs the length of the Atlantic Ocean, is often cited by Atlantean researchers as being a remnant of the lost continent. However, the ridge is now known to be rising, not sinking, through volcanic and seismic action. However, that doesn't mean there's nothing left to discover: In 2023, scientists completed mapping a previously unknown undersea continent, known as Zealandia, which covers more than 2 million square miles (5.1 million sq km) around New Zealand and Tasmania. This so-called "eighth continent" really did sink under the ocean—but 80 million years ago, when dinosaurs still roamed.

OPPOSITE: Some say the craterlike Richat Structure, or Eye of the Sahara, in northwestern Africa was the site of Atlantis.

POSEIDON

to archaeology. Competition is still part of the profession, but in the few decades since Marinatos made his remark, the tools of archaeology have advanced far beyond spades. Satellite photos guided the Spanish workers in the Doñana wetlands. Remote-operated vehicles can explore nearly 4 miles (6.4 km) beneath the seas, a depth that brings 98 percent of the ocean floor within reach. Magnetometers, which measure magnetic forces and changes in magnetic fields, can detect in fine detail where soils have been moved, replaced, and resettled. Ground-penetrating radar can glimpse buried structures. Laser scanning can help researchers develop 3D images of structures in far greater detail than photography would.

Of course, some of the basic chores of archaeology remain unchanged. Artifacts are still pulled from dirt, rock, muck, and roots. They must be laboriously washed by hand, labeled, and stored. In much the same way, the search for Atlantis is likely to continue, even as Plato's 2,000-year-old story meets the powerful new technologies of the 21st century. Atlantis remains one of humankind's great mysteries—a potential connection between humans and gods such as Zeus and Poseidon. Finding it remains a scientific challenge and a logical puzzle, because, while no one has proven that Atlantis ever truly existed, no one will ever be able to prove that it didn't.

TODAY AND TOMORROW

45

FIELD NOTES

archaeologist—a person who studies human history by examining ancient people and their artifacts

embalm—to prevent the decay of a body by treating it with preservatives

geologist—a scientist who studies the physical components of Earth

occult—mysterious, hidden, or otherwise unexplainable by science

philosopher—a person who examines or develops systems of beliefs

pseudoscience—beliefs or practices which are mistakenly or fraudulently thought to be based on solid scientific principles

reincarnation—the return of a being who has died in the form of another person or animal

seismic—having to do with earthquakes

skeptical—doubtful

sonar—a technique using sound waves to navigate, find, or communicate with other objects under water

telepathy—communication of thoughts or ideas through means other than the known senses

tomb-raider—a person who steals ancient artifacts and even human remains

utopia—a community that is perfect or ideal

Western—having a culture connected to European and Christian traditions as well as those based in ancient Greece and Rome

SELECTED BIBLIOGRAPHY

Adams, Mark. *Meet Me in Atlantis: My Obsessive Quest to Find the Sunken City*. New York: Dutton, 2015.

Ashe, Geoffrey. *Atlantis: Lost Lands, Ancient Wisdom*. New York: Thames and Hudson, 1992.

Castleden, Rodney. *Atlantis Destroyed*. London; New York: Routledge, 1998.

De Camp, L. Sprague. *Lost Continents: The Atlantis Theme in History, Science, and Literature*. New York: Dover Publications, 1970.

Jordan, Paul. *The Atlantis Syndrome*. Stroud, England: Sutton, 2003.

King, David. *Finding Atlantis: A True Story of Genius, Madness, and an Extraordinary Quest for a Lost World*. New York: Harmony Books, 2005.

WEBSITES

Plato
https://www.history.com/topics/ancient-greece/plato
Read about the philosopher's life, dialogues, and lasting legacy.

Sunken Cities
https://www.livescience.com/real-life-atlantis-settlements.html
Discover other cities throughout history that have vanished into the sea.

INDEX

Africa, 23, 25, 26, 27, 32, 38, 41
Aristotle, 21
Ashe, Geoffrey, 19
Atlantic Ocean, 12, 13, 18, 25, 26, 41, 43
Atlantis
    age, 10
    empire, 12
    landscape, 13, 14
    name origin, 13
    people (Atlanteans), 9, 12, 13, 14, 19, 21,
        24, 25, 33, 34
    rulers, 10, 12, 13, 14
Bacon, Sir Francis, 23
Benoit, Pierre, 29
Berlioux, Etienne Felix, 27, 29
Bernard, Raymond, 35
Blavatsky, Helena Petrovna ("Madame"),
        30, 31
    and Theosophical Society, 31
Burroughs, Edgar Rice, 30
Cayce, Edgar, 33, 34
Critias, 10, 18
de Camp, L. Sprague, 21
Doggerland, 26
Doñana National Park, Spain, 42, 45
Donnelly, Ignatius, 24, 25, 27, 31, 33
Doyle, Sir Arthur Conan, 30
earthquakes, 9, 12, 14, 19, 33, 38, 43
Europe, 23, 24, 26, 32, 42
Evans, Sir Arthur, 37, 38
floods, 14, 18, 24, 26
Freund, Richard, 42
Greek islands
    Crete, 37, 38, 41
    Santorini, 38, 40, 41, 42
    Thera. *See* Santorini
Greek mythology
    Atlas, 13
    minotaur, 38
    Poseidon, 12, 14, 45
    Theseus, 38
    Zeus, 14, 37, 45
Hörbiger, Hanns, 33

Howard, Robert E., 30
Kalokairinos, Minos, 37
Khun de Prorok, Count Byron, 27
King, David, 24
Knossos, Crete, 18, 37, 38, 41
Lovecraft, H. P., 30
Marinatos, Spyridon, 38, 42, 45
Mediterranean Sea, 12, 23, 26, 27, 41, 42
Mid-Atlantic Ridge, 24, 43
Minoans, 18, 38, 42
Mount Shasta, 34
Nazis, 32
New World, 21, 23
Oliver, Frederick Spencer, 34
Pacific Ocean, 16, 23, 41
Pillars of Heracles, 12, 13, 24, 41
Plato, 10, 12, 13, 14, 17, 18, 19, 21, 23, 25, 26,
        33, 38, 41, 42, 45
popular culture
    books, 24, 29, 30, 31
    comics, 30
    movies, 30, 31
Richat Structure (Eye of the Sahara), 45
Rock of Gibraltar, 13
Roux, Claude, 27
Rudbeck, Olof, 23, 24
Socrates, 10, 17, 18
South America, 23, 25, 33
Strait of Gibraltar, 12, 23, 24, 26, 41, 42
Sweden, 23, 24
Symmes, John Cleves, 34, 35
Timaeus, 10, 18
Tolkien, J. R. R., 30
Tschoegl, Nicholas, 41
Tyree, J. M., 27
Verne, Jules, 24, 29
volcanoes, 16, 19, 33, 41, 43
Woods Hole Oceanographic Institution, 16
    research vessels, 16
Zealandia, 43